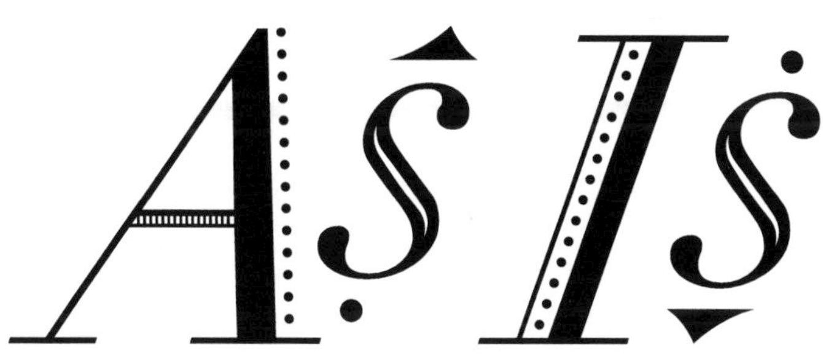

A 21 Day Practice for Finding a Home and Peace in Your Skin

Contents

To the reader:

If you are receiving this book as a gift it is because someone loves you very much. It's possible they are not sure you see yourself as the beautiful, important person you are. I hope you view this book it as the gift it is meant to be. It is intended to help you unravel ideas about yourself that don't serve you. If you are giving yourself this gift, congratulations! Perhaps this little book can be the road-map that helps you find your way home to yourself. Inviting a new reality is an empowering step toward loving yourself. It is my hope that this book serves to reveal to you your own light—that you might learn to be compassionate with yourself and others in a way that will forever change your life. There is life beyond the certainty and fear that something is wrong with you. My life began when my primary question stopped being "Am I beautiful enough?" or even "Am I enough?" and became "Am I living a beautiful life?" My wish for you is the same.

About the author:

I started blogging in 2010 when I started a personal training business. At the time, becoming a personal trainer seemed completely outrageous. It didn't align with all of the things I had long believed about myself. It didn't fit my identity. I had spent my whole life feeling like my body was all wrong. Aside from some brief bouts of physical activity in junior high sports (that mostly consisted of a slew of embarrassing stories of spectacular non-athleticism), I was largely inactive. My eating habits were poor at best. And even though I had just spent a year turning around my physical and mental health, it was really hard to identify as a personal trainer or athlete. At the time, I was trying to decide whether or not to go back to school and toying around with what I might do. I spent all of my evenings pouring over training plans and excited about exercise. I remember showing my little sister all of the plans I was working on and she sort of gasped at how much energy and passion I was putting into my work. It was she who first suggested I become a personal trainer – and as a birthday present that year she created my first website (fitmamatraining.com) and told me to go start my business. It was such a loving move, but I was terrified. I didn't want anyone to know about it. Her husband set up my first Facebook page (now Facebook.com/iamerinbown). I was so worried! People would know?! I felt like a fraud. Who would listen to *me*? What could I possibly have to say? Wouldn't everyone just laugh at me? But I knew deep down that having a business and trying to keep it a secret didn't really make sense. I would like to think that without those initial "pushes" I would still be doing what I do today, but the truth is, everything I do now is because I was thrown into it by my loving family. In 2014, I changed my Facebook platform from Fit Mama Training to "I am Erin Brown" because I realized I had never used my website or my social media platforms to promote my fitness training business. Moreover, my client training work had always been much more centered on helping people make paradigm shifts about their bodies than it was about actual body shaping. All of my work had become about confidence, letting go of shame, and empowering people to live in the bodies they have while learning how to view exercise and food choices as self-care.

At the time, I was experiencing a lot of "backlash" online. My Facebook page was gaining what felt like overwhelming momentum with thousands of new people "liking" my page each day. I went from having what felt like a supportive online community to ever-present and disturbing online attacks. I decided that "Fit Mama Training" was attracting people who were seeking "Fitness!" + "Moms!" messaging, but who were then disappointed when I didn't propagate the typical headless abdominal photos with inspirational quotes about fat "crying" (sweat = fat crying). It felt like a good time to make some changes. Today I no longer take on personal training clients. Instead, I focus on body and life empowerment through writing, workshops and speaking engagements.

I hope this book allows you to begin to experience the shifts in thinking that changed my life. Smaller pants didn't change my life. Being physically fit *does* make my life easier. What's made the biggest difference is deciding to stop bullying myself all the time. I went from being my own worst enemy to taking care of myself in a way that is life-affirming every day. In order to do that, I had to believe I *deserved* that sort of care. My wish for you is to begin finding that you deserve it too. While I truly love exercise now (something I would have thought impossible in my past), my passion has always been about helping others connect with themselves and their bodies in positive ways. More information about me can be found at iamerinbrown.com. Thank you for reading; I am grateful for your consideration of my words.

Introduction:

The very idea of reading a book dedicated to feeling good about my body would have sounded ridiculous to me at one time. My thought process would have gone something like this: "*My body is awful. So it's nice that someone wrote a book about how to love their body but mine just isn't lovable. I can't imagine what kind of self-helpy crap this must be! What has to change is my thighs, not my mind.*"

So just know that if you are all the way over **there**, in that place where you feel your body is some measure of your worth, and you just don't have a good one...I understand. I spent the better part of my life hating my body. I was disengaged from it. I didn't know if I was full or hungry unless I was stuffed or ravenous. I was tired. I couldn't walk up a flight of stairs without getting winded. I hated every ounce of myself. And as I hated myself, I watched those ounces climb. The last time I looked at my scale, at my heaviest, I weighed 240 pounds. I couldn't bear to watch after that. So I didn't. And then I got pregnant and grew and grew even more.

I don't know what it was about 240 pounds, but it seems everyone has a "dreaded number." Something they can tell themselves "at LEAST I'm not **there.**" I remember staring at that number and feeling completely overwhelmed. I had successfully lost weight in the past, mostly by being hungry all the time and "binging" on exercise, but 240 pounds seemed insurmountable. At that point, I didn't even want to leave the house. I felt like a lazy slob. I was embarrassed for my husband, who I felt didn't sign up for all this weight gain. I was ashamed of myself and I was ashamed for him. I literally thought if I left the house everyone would laugh at me. I hit a wall and felt there was no way to come back again.

No one really knew about this either. I wasn't declining invites with "I'm too fat to leave the house right now, sorry." I also thought that the only thing that could possibly be worse than being morbidly obese was to complain and draw attention to it. So this shame I was living in was kept a close secret.

For me it was actually being pregnant that forced me to come "home" to my body. I had hated it so much for so long that I had disconnected myself from it. I treated it like the enemy. But when the enemy was carrying my child, I knew I had to start respecting it. It was someone else's home as well. I started eating healthier. I started moving.

If you are familiar with me and my story, this is the part where I lost 100 pounds. But that isn't the real story. I was larger and then I became smaller. I am now physically more comfortable in my body. I can run up a flight (or more) of stairs easily. That is good for my life. But the real transformation happened at the very beginning. And you don't have to be pregnant to transform your thinking. What happened is that I came to love and accept my body as my home, exactly as it was. At 240 pounds.

What happened is that I came to love and accept my body as my home, exactly as it was. At 240 pounds.

In the subsequent years my weight would fluctuate as my habits did. While I have never stopped exercising regularly or eating well, when the seasons change my exercise changes, and my body follows. Sometimes I am leaner and sometimes I am stronger and sometimes I'm curvier. I'm getting older. I have more years of strength training under my belt. There are a billion reasons my body continues to change. The biggest transformation I have ever made for my life was to love and accept my body the way it is, today. And tomorrow. And last year and next year. One day, universe willing, I will be very old. My skin will wrinkle. Perhaps I'll shrink like aging people tend to do. My ears will keep growing. My nose may grow. I will still love them. Because I know I deserve my own love and it is not at all contingent on the momentary details of my physical form. I realize that is a tall order, but when I finally gave myself a break and let go of all my shame, I allowed myself to finally ask the question "Am I living a beautiful life?" and not "Am I beautiful enough?" I cannot tell you how much happier I am for that shift. I could never go back.

For my own daughter, I would never want to teach her that any part of her was less important or unworthy.

So how did I get there?

First I should tell you that I still struggle. Every day is a day that I wake up and choose deliberately to love myself rather than hate myself. All the parts of myself. I know that some people find a sort of peace in separating their physical from their mental/spiritual bodies. These people say things about "beauty on the inside" which is, of course, true. You cannot love your physical body and be a mean/terrible/angry/judgmental person and still be a healthy person. But when I separated my body from my "self," I wasn't really honoring all the parts of me. For my own daughter, I would never want to teach her that any part of her was less important or unworthy. So I consciously decide to spend time taking care of my mind, my spirit and my body. Honoring and loving each of those parts of my "self," wherever they are, each day.

It's about living fully, with confidence in all the parts of me.

Here's how it works: when I feel stressed out, I take time to identify the stress, address it, and calm the heck down. Likewise, when I'm feeling icky about my body, I spend time working on it. This is something I have taught myself to do. I had to learn this. It is something I hope to pass on, perhaps covertly, to my daughter. She is likely to adopt the behavior I model. For me, this isn't just about "being body positive!" (Insert unicorn and rainbows here!), but about being honest and real with myself. It's about living fully, with confidence in all the parts of me. It's about continuing to thrive and grow as a person instead of having my whole life clouded by some ancient beliefs that something (anything) about me is disgusting or even just "meh." These ancient beliefs are old ideas and perceptions that aren't based in fact and no longer serve me.

This book is a guide to my consciousness-building practices. Some of the things I do will likely seem odd or uncomfortable to you. I ask that you simply consider them. To get different results you have to do different things. The work is to undo the years of messages, overt and subliminal, given to you by others and most importantly yourself. The work is to move on from notions about yourself that don't serve you. Decide something new and true about yourself. It will require work in your mind and spirit to embrace and care for your body.

This is a workbook. Each day there is a practice, a reason for it and some work for you to do with yourself. Also included are questions for journaling. I would recommend doing those at the end of the day, if it suits you. If something doesn't resonate with you, perhaps the next practice will. Some days you may want to spend more time on an exercise. Maybe you will need to repeat a day or two. The pace is up to you.

While I know all of our journeys are different, I also know from years of talking with people about their bodies that much of our struggles are the same. It is my hope that in being honest about my old stories, and my new stories, that you might find some keys to unlocking your own.

day *01*

Your Body is a Good Body

For today, I want you to consider that your body is not the problem. Your body is a good body. Even as I sit here on what feels like a mountain of confidence compared to the valley of self-despair I used to feel about my body, writing that sentence brings up some resistance in me. Your body is a good body. Yet I know it is true.

I have known a thousand different "kinds" of women. That is, they have all different kinds of bodies. What almost every one of them has in common is the disgust and disapproval they have for their bodies. It's such a "normal" thing that I didn't realize how normal it was until the first time I heard a woman say she was beautiful. I was twenty-one. I belonged to a group in college that traveled and did community service together. We were doing a "get to know you" activity on the first day. For the activity, we were given small pieces of paper and the presenter called out words like "hometown," "race," "gender," and "appearance." For each word called out, we were asked to write down how we defined ourselves using one word. Then we "ranked" each of the words in order of their perceived importance to us.

On my "appearance" card, I wrote "meh." (Meh is a Yiddish word that means "so-so"). I ranked it at the bottom in importance. This both reflected my struggle to believe that, "no, my appearance is not an important part of who I am," and my real belief that there was nothing special or noteworthy about how I looked. I found my appearance unacceptable. So I shoved that part of me all the way to the bottom of the stack. Another woman in the group wrote "beautiful" on her appearance card and ranked it at the top in importance. If your inclination is to judge her or think her vain, I beg to differ. She *was* beautiful. There are lots of ways to be beautiful. She explained herself by saying, "I am beautiful and I think that's important." She then went on to share other things about herself that were also beautiful. She was confident in herself, not in her ability to measure up to others.

It struck a chord in me and it still does. That group allowed me to travel the world and to do and see remarkable things, but hearing a mid-western farm girl call herself beautiful somehow remains the top-drawer memory from that experience. Meanwhile, the rest of the women I knew never went a day without lamenting some part of their body.

Meanwhile, the rest of the women I knew never went a day without lamenting some part of their body.

Getting dressed was a chore that involved a lot of looking in the mirror and wishing to see something different. All the women I knew did this. The thin ones, the ones with incredible muscles, the ones who worked out, the ones who didn't. Every size and shape of woman I knew found fault in her body. I realized two key things: One, I was not the only one who felt this way. The dark places in my head that I went to when I picked apart and hated every part of my body, feeling terribly alone, were the same dark places other women were going. And while we sometimes talked about it, we were just wallowing there instead of lifting each other up. We bumped into each other in the dark, but didn't help each other find the exit.

Self-hate will not go away if you make a physical change (i.e., lose weight). What grows from love, though, remains in love.

Two, it wasn't my body that needed to change. Yes, I was out of shape and not treating my body with respect. I deserved to gift to myself my own time, attention and care with regard to my body. But because I could see that women of all shapes and sizes loved and/or hated their appearance, I found that the difference between the ones who were at peace and the ones who were at war was their *perspective* and not their diet plan.

I want you to consider that the issues that you have with

your body and the way you look are not about your body. You didn't get a "bad" one. You don't need it to change for you to find peace and love for it. My primary goal is to pull you out of the space where you think you need to "fix" something about yourself to feel whole. Any habits you create in an effort to change your body so that you can elevate your worth, will come from a place of self-hate. Self-hate will not go away if you make a physical change (i.e., lose weight). What grows from love, though, remains in love.

When I made the shift from thinking my body was a sad sack of ugly to choosing to feel peaceful in my "home," I was floored by how often I was having negative thoughts. I knew I was disgusted with myself but I thought I was just having a perfectly reasonable response to being disgusting. When I became mindful of my thoughts, I realized I was bullying myself. I would talk to myself in a way I would never speak to another human being. It's not a stretch to say I was obsessed with bullying myself. It was chronic. The first step for me was becoming mindful of my self-talk.

Each day will offer something to be mindful of. A sentence or an idea to be thinking about as you travel through your day. If you are a person who meditates or likes think of this kind of work as meditation - awesome. If you are not, perhaps think about it as you are making your coffee and then again mid-day and before your evening meal. I'm not concerned about what you call this practice, but I will call it mindfulness practice.

Mindfulness Practice Day 01:

Notice the way you talk to yourself. When you get dressed are you being kind or cruel to yourself in the mirror? Are you happy? Are you upset? Are you weighing yourself and feeling overly excited or sad? Are you attaching some part of your confidence or emotional state to that number on the scale? Are you afraid of the scale but think about it whenever you are in the bathroom?

Just notice.

And as you are noticing your thoughts, if anything negative comes up simply say aloud or in your mind, "I can choose peace." This of course doesn't mean you are instantly curing yourself of your negative thought patterns and old gremlins. But just give yourself a gentle nudge that you could choose to feel peaceful. "I can choose peace" doesn't mean your thighs will look different by noon, or that you will find yourself enamored with your breasts by morning.

"I can choose peace" means just that. Choosing a peaceful feeling in your body. Thoughts are powerful and you get to choose them. The first step toward owning that power is noticing them.

Journal Day 01:

How often are you bullying yourself? Are there parts of day or activities that trigger a negative thought process? What kind of things are you saying to yourself? How would you feel if someone was saying those things to your best friend? Your kid? (literal or figurative).

day 02

"Girl Talk"

As you went about your first day being mindful, you may have found that negative body talk came up both when you were alone and when you were with others. Since hating our bodies is such a common practice we often have people in our lives with whom we share this habit. For the most part, I liked to keep my self-hatred to myself. I must have read in a magazine at some point that "confidence is sexy" and decided that fake confidence was my best shot at being considered attractive. So I went about masking my insecurity with pronounced fake confidence. But I still found that I constantly heard other people (usually women) say disparaging things about themselves and others.

The one time I remember really "bonding" with another woman over our disgust for ourselves happened in college. I had a roommate who was also obsessed with her size, which she of course considered "too big." We laid on her bed staring at the ceiling taking turns picking ourselves apart.

She would lament about a body part and we would laugh and then I would take a turn. While there was a strange liberation in declaring aloud how I felt about myself, I definitely didn't leave that conversation feeling better. I remember thinking she must have agreed with the things I'd said. I felt more certain than ever that something was wrong with me.

Just the other day I was at my kid's soccer game sitting next to someone's grandmother. We talked about kids and sunscreen and then, out of nowhere, she started apologizing to me for being fat. With a friend or peer I might have responded with: "I wish you saw yourself like I do" or "don't talk about my friend like that!" But with a complete stranger I wasn't prepared. So I said nothing. Right then, my daughter joined us and I diverted my attention to her. If I had it to do over again, I still wouldn't have participated in her self-criticism, but I would have found something to say. Perhaps: "I understand how you feel, it's just not what I focus my life on anymore." I no longer believe it's healthy for me or for you to encourage self-hatred.

I walked away from that interaction feeling sad for her, but on a macro scale, discouraged for all of us. How common place has this shared self-disgust become when women out of no where apologize for their bodies? To strangers? I've found these kind of conversations the most difficult to keep from my daughter's young consciousness. While many continue to point at the media for young girl's obsession with weight, it's the words of the women around her I struggle the most to keep from impacting my girl.

My final example is the most common tale. In my work as a fitness trainer, most women I meet sit down with me and within the first five minutes declare that they need to lose "about 20 pounds." Not that it makes a difference here, but these women's bodies are always very different. Somehow they all believe they need to lose at least 20 pounds.

It upsets me when a woman I admire goes out of her way to tell me what is "wrong" with her size. In one form or another it's a way of apologizing for her appearance, for the way that she "is." An apology I don't believe anyone needs to make. Ever.

It's not that I think wanting to lose weight is the worst goal or topic of conversation anyone could desire. But something has got to change in our world when fat is the primary topic women talk about together. Our bodies have become our shared torment and prisons instead of our homes.

These conversations are not uplifting. They further the agreement that we have to be a particular way or size to be valuable or loved. It is worth considering if these conversations are the best use of your time and energy.

Mindfulness Practice Day 02:

Notice how the people around you talk about their bodies. When you're with others, are there comments about the calorie content of food? Is there a candy jar at work? Do people make comments about how "bad" they are for eating from it? Just being a part of others' conversations about themselves can reinforce the negative talk in our own minds. I don't want you go about your day looking for negative or body-conscious conversations. Just notice how and when the topics of bodies, size, calories, fat, attractiveness, and weight come up. Notice how you *feel* and react. Notice how you feel when someone else is being disparaging or, contrastingly, uplifting to themselves. Today take a small step back from your normal participation in the candy jar conversations and observe what's going on and the impact it has on you. If you feel uncomfortable, return to the mantra "I can choose peace."

Journal Day 02:

How did negative body talk come up for you today? Were you surprised how often it happened? How did you feel noticing it? Was it hard to observe?

day *03*

Stop participating

It can be hard to pull away from body-negative, calorie-obsessed conversations, especially if you work in a place where folks eat lunch together. I don't know which is sadder to me, how typical it has become to sit around a table and make shameful comments about eating, or the fact that I hadn't noticed how commonplace the shameful eating comments had become? It's such an accepted experience that it's easy to not take notice when you are doing it yourself. Breaking bread with friends should not be such an emotionally daunting or judgmental event.

Not willing to outwardly admit my insecurities, I used to make a lot of jokes at my own expense. Many of these would occur at mealtimes. "I'm just going to pig out" I'd laugh, or I'd explain my full plate by commenting that I "hadn't eaten anything at all today." There was lots of talk about dieting. Always. In retrospect all of these conversations can be summed up with this statement: "I am feeling really insecure."

It's all I was ever really saying about my body.

There are so many reasons I don't want to live in that space anymore.

I don't want my life to be about dieting anymore. I have a finite amount of energy each day. I don't want to distract from anything or anyone or any moment I have to love by being unkind or downright mean to myself. The quality of my life is bigger than my thighs. And I live accordingly.

I have a little girl who is watching me. She pays attention to every darn thing I do. I know that my inner voice will one day become her own. I take that seriously. I will not teach her to spend her energy picking apart her body. I refuse to pass that on to her.

I don't agree that the worth of my life is contingent upon the appearance of my body. I don't believe that is true for anyone.

So I won't participate in conversations that contradict my vision for my life. I won't for myself. I won't for the sake of the person I'm talking to. This transition may take some getting used to, for you and others, but everyone will get used to the change. I know sometimes my friends have to pause before they say things about their bodies to me because they have become more mindful about how they speak of themselves around me. Not because I'll scold them, but because I won't jump on the "Yeah, let's all lose 20 pounds" bandwagon, nor will I agree about how "bad" we are for indulging. I just simply don't.

You may even feel like you are letting someone down if you aren't doing what you have always done. We all know these comments and conversations only lead to more negativity. For everyone involved. What you give energy to, grows. If you give energy to mocking, ridiculing or shaming bodies, then mockery, ridicule and shame grows.

Mindfulness Practice Day 3:

Actively disengage from speaking ill about your body in conversations where others are doing it. It's just one day. (You can do it!) It might be surprising how often the topic comes up. It's one thing to stop yourself from talking about your body, but not to participate with others can be a real challenge. So a few suggestions to get you through the day if you find yourself in a conversation where someone is lamenting their beautiful, functional skin:

1. *It makes me sad to hear you say that.*
2. *I think we've all learned to be unnecessarily hard on ourselves.*
3. *It's hard, but I'm really trying to be more positive in the way I talk about myself.*

None of this has to do with weight loss. It's about not fueling a conversation that is really just bullying. No one needs to be bullied by themselves. And you don't have to participate.

Journal Day 3:

Is it more uncomfortable to not participate in bullying conversations that to jump in? Why? What would it feel like to not have these conversations anymore?

day 04

OPP (Other People's Opinions)

I have lived and nearly died by the opinions of others. It's sort of weird and cathartic to share such personal confessions, but I believe there is great meaning in our shared experiences. So I am very open about my own. I don't remember when it was that I started hating my body. I do remember quitting ballet when I was four years old because I felt my thighs were too big. At the time, all I wanted was to be a dancer but I had somehow absorbed the message from the constantly dieting women around me that my body wasn't good enough. No one in the ballet program was actively teaching the girls about dieting, but I was already emulating the body hatred I saw around me and judging my own body against the weight and size and contours of my peers. **At four years old, I felt the need to shut down parts of myself to apologize for my body.** The first dream to go, was my dream of becoming a ballerina. Surely, I thought, my body was not ballerina material.

I don't know if you know many four year olds but that's a pretty fun and innocent age. While I call myself a "body image expert," what I really am is a "self-hate expert." I have spent so much time exploring every corner of that particular hell I feel like a tour guide. Like many experts, I got started on my research very early.

Interestingly, I don't think any of those ashamed thoughts were my own creation. I didn't somehow reach my own conclusion at the ripe old age of four that there was something wrong with me. I didn't decide that being physically beautiful, by being thin in the "perfect" way, was the ultimate lifetime goal of Erin Brown. This was an obsession that was handed to me, if you will, by osmosis (otherwise known as: my mother, my grandmother, other women in my life, perhaps television and casually overheard conversations). And as I came to believe this "ugly truth" with every part of my being, I sought out mirrors that reflected my skewed view of female perfection. When they say that optimists and pessimists are both right, this is what they mean.

We constantly seek proof that our perceptions are reality. As I came to embrace the belief that something was inherently wrong and ugly about my body - I found evidence of my ugliness everywhere.

Unfortunately, there are entire, gigantic industries capitalizing on the idea that we should (or do) hate ourselves. They profit from it in a big way! Diet commercials, magazines, gym memberships, home-training equipment, the pill-of-the month club – all that stuff is marketed in such a way that not only promises rapid weight loss (which is the *BEST* thing you could ever do with your entire life! *note sarcasm) but you will finally be so happy. You'll get the house, the boat, the house-boat, and all the dreams you've ever had at the other side of the perfect body rainbow.

It's exhausting to think about how frequent and pervasive these messages have become. Not only do these messages come from the media, they come from friends, co-workers, family members, your childhood, your ex-lover, and virtually any comment anyone has ever made to you about your body. "Hey, you've lost weight! Congratulations!" But none of those opinions, views or ideologies have to become yours.

I learned to diet from my mother. Simply by watching her diet. I don't think for a minute that learning to diet by watching someone else do it has to suggest anything about my body – or about how much my mother loves me. I have the best mother in the world. I was just emulating how she felt about herself. She had no idea her feelings about her own body were having a negative effect on me. The ex-boyfriend who broke up with me because "my weight was bad for his reputation" was only poisonous to me because I agreed with him. Had he picked something to criticize about me with which I didn't agree so whole-heartedly, I would not have felt the pain so acutely. He pointed out my biggest insecurity and it cut like a knife. What I have learned is that the ugliness of his overheard remark had everything to do with him and his journey of self-acceptance, and nothing at all to do with me. When another woman makes a nasty remark about my body (as an online personality, you can imagine that this happens all the time) I now know for certain that her comment has to do with what's going on inside her and not something bad or wrong with me.

Once I made the deliberate choice to be at peace with my body exactly as it is at any moment, it became clear that the things I would hear from others about my body had nothing at all to do with me. How could they? Ironically, having all of the "online commentary" about my body has actually helped me detach completely from others' opinions. I found that the exact same photo of me in a bikini would elicit diametrically opposed feedback. The same photo! Either, "You are so lucky, I'd kill to have a body like yours" or "I don't know why you think you deserve to be a fitness professional, I would never want to look like you." These opposing comments on the same photo tell me nothing about me, and a whole lot about the person making the comment.

Mindfulness Practice Day 4:

When you receive feedback about your body from others today, notice how it feels. Does positive feedback feel amazing? Does negative feedback feel like the end of the world? Neither the positive nor the negative input is really yours to own; it belongs to the sender. For today, notice how it feels in your body. Consider the new reality that this feedback reflects the other person entirely – and notice how it feels. Is it loving? Is it helpful?

Journal Day 4

What would you do if you knew no one would judge you for it? What's stopping you?

day 05

Nothing's personal

Everyone has baggage. Everyone has sad stories they carry around, some dating to early childhood. Taking time to be introspective can help you identify and unpack the baggage, but not everyone does that. Lots of people walk around sharing their baggage with others by way of judgments and other unhealthy behaviors. Some people do this all day long. But these judgments aren't yours, even if they are directed at you.

Embarrassingly, I have spent a lot of time picking apart other women. If any of these women heard the things I said to my friends or thought in my mind, I'd be devastated. I was hyper-critical in every way because I believed that bringing others down a notch would make me feel better.

My baggage, you ask? My "old story" is that I'm invisible and don't matter. I tied this story to everything in my life. Instead of dealing with myself, I tried to pick apart the women I thought were visible and mattered. The ones people paid attention to. The ones guys liked. The ones my exes liked.

My judgments had NOTHING to do with them and everything to do with ME. I was projecting outwardly what was within me – and what I said to myself.

I feel really fortunate to have made this discovery long before my Facebook page grew to almost 100,000 "likes," because the internet is chock full of feedback. While I realized that sharing as openly as I do would leave me vulnerable to criticism, nothing could have really prepared me for the sort of comments people evidently feel comfortable writing when they feel anonymous. I have been called ugly, fat, disgusting and stupid. I have been emailed on numerous occasions by men letting me know whether or not they would have sex with me. I have been told I should "never expect a man to still be there in the morning" because I was so unattractive. Once, a woman spent an entire day commenting on a post I wrote about finding joy. Her comment was that I should be ashamed of my body – never joyful. That I believe in body peace as a means of "justifying" the way I look.

My judgments had NOTHING to do with them and everything to do with ME. I was projecting outwardly what was within me – and what I said to myself.

Most of the feedback I get is positive but the negative sure has a way of sounding so much louder. Most days the negative personal feedback doesn't bother me. Most days I send up a little blessing for that person's self-worth. I hope that they can eventually come to a place where they let go of the need to send out such negative energy. I acknowledge that someone can only give what they have inside of them.

I've no interest in knowing who would pursue having sex

with me. I don't agree that having a body, or having a public body on the internet, begs that question. I don't agree that I'm ugly, disgusting or stupid. I don't *agree,* so I brush it off. I have had a lot of practice. But there are days when someone says something that really touches a soft spot and I find myself confronted by my old story: "I am invisible and I don't matter."

I had a personal experience recently which revived my old story. There is a woman I encounter regularly; we have a few mutual friends but we are not close. Whenever we would run into each other, she seemed short with me, and she never remembered who I was (and she was introduced to me dozens of times). She was cold, it seemed. Also, I'm a regular at *her* business which would seem to guarantee me some level of recognition or grace. This drove me nuts! I felt so *dismissed* by her.

I was recounting one of these interactions to a mutual friend and she dropped this woman's story on me. Like a ton of bricks. Her personal details have no place here, but she is a woman with a long history of personal trauma. Trauma I wouldn't wish on anyone. Trauma that may well result in not relating well to others and putting up huge emotional walls. "How you feel about me is between you and your self-esteem" is something I talk and write about often. And yet I was taking this woman's dismissal personally when it had to do with *my* baggage. Nothing is personal. Her behavior made me feel invisible. But that is mine to deal with.

Just when I thought I'd learned this particular message it came up for me again when an old co-worker opened a butcher shop in my neighborhood. Being established by a local guy and featuring all locally sourced product, it was a shop I was excited to frequent. I found myself slightly miffed that every time I walked in and waved he ignored me. But I didn't allow myself the headspace to be upset about it and did my best not to take it personally. This went on for a few weeks when he walked into the glasses store where I was working as an optician. He was very friendly. I asked him if these would be his first glasses, as I'd never seen him wear them in our years of knowing one another. He replied, "No. I just never, ever wear them and I really need to. People keep coming into my business and waving and I have no idea who they are. I can't see them."

Dang. I went about doing my job but I wanted to roll on the floor laughing. I get it. It's not about me. It so very rarely ever is.

It's on those days, when you feel invisible or dismissed, that today's practice is the most useful. Instead of dealing with how someone else has "made me feel," I deal with my own junk. Am I agreeing with the criticism I'm sure is directed at me? Could this be an important critique for me to learn from? Is it loving and intended for my growth? Or, most likely, is this something I am feeling insecure about?

When someone says or does something that makes you feel bad, it stings. Especially if that person is close to you. More so, if they are hitting you in a soft spot. But in either case, it's best to deal with yourself, and remember that if someone is being intentionally hurtful they are putting out what they have to give. It's not always yours to own.

I get it. It's not about me. It so very rarely ever is.

There have been a few days when I've had to remove myself completely from my role as an "online personality" and just run or hike or meditate on a comment. Days like that don't happen often but I take the business of addressing and respecting my inner self quite seriously. I "hold on to it" to see if it's really "mine." Is the criticism something I need to work on? An area where I need some growth? If it's not, I contemplate the following mindfulness practice.

Mindfulness Practice Day 5:

Let other people keep their "stuff." Don't take it on or shoulder the load if it's not yours. When someone says something disparaging about you, or when some outside force seems to be telling you something is "wrong" with you, let it go. Don't take the comment personally or agree. Don't *receive* it. Don't attach it to yourself as the badge you have to wear today. Just notice that any incoming message is attached to something outside of you. Just for today, observe it and let it go. Oftentimes, if it feels too heavy, it's because it isn't yours.

Journal Day 5:

What stuff have you been carrying around with you? How does it feel? Is it heavy? Is it overwhelming? Is it even yours? What steps can you take to let it go?

day 06

Who asked you?

Here is one thing I know for sure: people who are confident do not run around being overly critical of others. Being critical of others is an excellent way to express to others that you are insecure and critical of yourself. Just as criticism evolves from your insecurities, it also amplifies your self-doubt.

Being critical of others is an excellent way to express to others that you are insecure and critical of yourself.

I have historically been terrible about criticism. Ever-convinced that there was something wrong with me, I picked apart others as well as myself. It's as if I believed it would make me feel better to notice all the flaws in someone else's body. I wanted to wrap myself in a security blanket woven from the knowledge that other women weren't perfect either.

I remember looking at photos on social media of my ex-boyfriend's new girlfriends and editing like it was my job. I would look at her face like it was an object for dissecting with my judgments. I'd compare her stomach to mine, or her stomach to the standard of "perfection." I'd get friends in on the action; I liked to have them tell me how much prettier I was. None of that dealt with the actual issue. I was feeling insecure, alone, and unwanted. What I needed in that moment was to realize she had nothing at all to do with me. I was mourning a relationship that didn't turn out the way I'd hoped. I needed to build myself up, not drag someone else down with me. In the end, I realized I couldn't rebuild my self-esteem on a foundation of critical judgment or false bravado.

I know I'm not alone. These days I hate to be anywhere near a social media outlet during the annual Victoria's Secret fashion show. The comments range from "My man would never want to be with a woman who looked like that," to "Gross! Eat a sandwich!" Some feign concern, but calling a body gross or "accusing" someone of having an eating disorder is not concern. Nor is it activism. Nor is it meant to be helpful in any way. All of these comments declare: "I am feeling wildly insecure."

"How you feel about *me* is between you and your self-esteem." This is a phrase I repeat often. I reflect on this quote to deflect other's judgments of me, and also to remind myself, when I'm feeling the need to judge another, that something must be going on inside *me* that I need to address. It goes both ways.

It requires a lot of work and energy to be hyper-critical of others. Ironically, it only ever made me feel worse. I realized that all the critical comments ever did was keep me in a hyper-critical state of myself and others. These comments furthered my dogma that bodies (including my own) were here for scrutiny and dissection. Nothing positive grows from all that negativity.

I realize that, by way of the exercises in this book, I'm asking you to consciously undo behaviors that may have become unconscious habits. It may seem unnatural or hard to change them. Consider that when the behavior you need to change affects your life in negative ways, then not changing is also hard.

I will tell you right now that it gets easier. New habits can and will be formed. How do I know? One of the most challenging things for me about writing this book was that I had to tap back into these old thought patterns. They are no longer second nature; I don't think like that anymore. It's not that I never have a judgmental thought or dislike something about myself, but rather that I acknowledge what is going on when something critical comes up and I deal with what is really happening inside of me. Adopting these mindfulness practices is about becoming conscious of your behavior to allow for your own growth. It isn't simple. But it is the sort of work that can make you a better person.

Mindfulness Practice Day 6:

Rather than justify your behavior today or even feel guilty about it, I want you to notice when you begin to think or say negative things about someone else's appearance. What about them made you want to comment? What feelings came up inside you that you need to address? Are you jealous? Do you relate to them? Are you angry?

If looking at someone else's body makes you angry - I'm sorry to tell you that that is your junk, not theirs. Other people have the right to look like they do and take up the space that they do. People on both extremes of thinness and largeness and everyone in between have the right to walk around in their bodies and if you find fault in that - you will always struggle with yourself as well. How could you not? If you spend your days criticizing everything about others' bodies, how could your own body ever compete to make the "good list?"

Just for today, notice what is going on inside of *you* when you find yourself being judgmental of someone else. Look for patterns. Be curious about your behavior and take note of what comes up.

Journal Day 6:

What patterns did you notice in your own thoughts? Did you find you were more or less critical than you thought? How do you feel about what you noticed?

day 07

The gift of not giving voice to every thought in your head

As you become curious about your "other-judgments" you will likely become quite aware of how often they arise. Today, I'd like you to stop giving them a voice. We have control over our thoughts but you aren't an awful person if a terrible one pops into your head. Especially if you are just now becoming mindful of what those thoughts even sound like.

If I find myself judging another person in any way, but for the sake of specificity let's say I'm judging another woman's body, I find an opportunity there. Rather than pick apart what is "wrong" with the other woman, I try to decipher what is happening within me. Am I feeling insecure? Am I upset about something? What is going on with *me* that I'm trying to soothe or deal with by dissecting *her?* But here's the trick: to have any shot at evolving I have to somehow stop giving voice to judgments.

I am not a saint. Nor am I asking you to become one. The primary argument I hear when I bring up this topic is: "What about _________ (fill in the blank)? Some types of people/body type/behavior are worthy of judgment!" What I'd like you to consider about this argument is how little it serves you. Having been a social worker for many years I met a lot of different kinds of people from different walks of life with a wide variety of stories and issues. I learned a lot about the "whys" of people's behavior. I evolved to have great compassion in the face of any behavior because there is likely so much behind it you cannot possibly know. Sometimes people's behavior does call us to action, but it doesn't inherently ask us to judge. Judgment primarily hurts the one doing it. It is not action based. When you judge someone, you're not helping them or yourself in any useful or loving way.

Most often, what is happening when we are judging others is this: we are responding to something we don't like about ourselves. Could it be you are judging some behavior that you yourself might be accused of? In some cases your judgments might be bringing up people or situations from your past from which you haven't healed. Regardless of the circumstances, I've simply found that my energy is best used drudging up what MY issue is and looking to resolve it rather than spew out some critical and unfounded comment about another human.

When you judge someone, you're not helping them or yourself in any useful or loving way.

And you know what? I still find it really difficult to be around certain people. Some people seem to "activate" parts of me that are easily irritable and frustrated. In those cases as well, I try to assess what is happening within ME so I will not lose my power or energy. As often as humanly possible, my goal is to use my energy in positive ways. So I offer compassion to others and then to myself. I ask myself what is wrong. I pause instead of react. And I hope to find my own healing in situations where I feel compelled to judge another. I find that this practice brings me peace rather than anxiety or anger or remorse for having judged. In Chapter 6 we established that we always see things as we are; if we see lack, it is because we feel that same lack within. However, I want to know how to bring myself peace and see beauty. It begins with stopping short of judgment, and learning to look at me.

Mindfulness Practice Day 7:

Stop giving voice to judgments. How? Practice. If you've been doing the same thing for a long time you probably feel like that is just "who you are." You may have decided you are critical by nature and do not have control. But you do. You just have to practice something new. Just for today, stop yourself before you voice aloud judgments about others. Notice what feelings are in your heart and in your body when these thoughts come up. Try to observe without judgment how you feel. Today, say to yourself, "this doesn't serve me or anyone" and then move on. Or spend time being curious with yourself about what is really causing your reaction. But for today, it doesn't get to have a voice. Giving your judgments a voice stops you from growing and accepting. Give yourself the gift of contemplation; take a pause and deal with yourself...and then move on.

Journal Day 7:

Was it hard to stop yourself short of making critical comments? Did you notice any patterns of when they came up (people, places, ways you were feeling at the time)? What did you find yourself replacing those comments with?

day 08

Collateral damage

Every single time I recall listening to someone make remarks about another person's body, I have immediately felt bad about my own. I would immediately scan the other woman's body, whether on television, in a magazine, or right before my eyes, and make somewhere in the neighborhood of 6,000 mental comparisons of her shape to my own. The result of hearing someone else bashed is to feel bad about myself. Always.

I consider this when I think about what kinds of words I want my daughter to hear come from my mouth. I think about what my words mean and what values and judgments I'm imparting to her when I use them. I might say to myself: "If I sit here and remark about (insert celebrity name)'s cellulite on this magazine cover, I am not only telling my daughter about the importance of not having cellulite, but that it is appropriate or even necessary that we remark about it." I might also be telling her that women exist to be stared at and categorized and evaluated. The list of messages I might be imparting in a moment like this is long. What might be happening is me feeling bad about me or the physical expectations I have for myself. Why else would I feel compelled to comment on (insert celebrity name)'s cellulite?

I no longer agree with the cultural assumption that women are here to be physically appealing to others. And I do my best to make sure my thoughts, my actions and my voice are reflective of that conviction.

I realize this perspective is not often considered. When a friend goes off on a diatribe about an acquaintance or even a celebrity's weight gain, for example, I know this is not a personal attack on me. But historically this does result in an immediate inner attack on myself. "If she feels this way about X, what must she think when she looks at me?!" "How do I compare to X?" And on and on and on. Of course you are not responsible for anyone's self-criticism. The only person who has control over what is happening in their heads is the individual at hand. But considering the possibility of collateral damage of our judgments might be the extra push you need to stop voicing them. It's not only bad for you, it's bad for everyone involved. And this too, is based on the agreement (that you don't have to subscribe to) that we are here to be looked at, scrutinized, and commented on. I no longer agree with the cultural assumption that women are here to be physically appealing to others. And I do my best to make sure my thoughts, my actions and my voice are reflective of that conviction.

When we give *voice* to our judgments we are often stuck in the insecurity we are experiencing in the moment. We don't consciously realize how our words are affecting others or ourselves. But poison is poison is poison. It's worth thinking for a moment about how your judgments affect others as well as yourself.

Mindfulness Practice Day 8:

If you are sharing judgments with others - you are hurting them. Even if you aren't sharing your criticism with the person you are talking about, you are causing harm. What most people hear when you talk about *any* body is their interpretation about what that might mean about *their* body (i.e. "If he thinks that about *her*, what must he think of *me*?")

Just as this kind of thinking or talking affects your ability to love and accept yourself, it does the same for everyone who hears it. If you find yourself wanting to talk negatively about someone else, keep it to yourself. Consider for today that negative judgments affect everyone you share them with. For today, spare others the self-judgment they'll feel as you criticize yourself or others.

Stopping the endless judgment and chatter about bodies can be challenging. Especially when there are others with whom you regularly dish gossip or trade barbs. But just as any kind of growth or change to your being meets a little resistance before it becomes accepted that "this is who you are now," eventually it will be old news that you don't participate in negative chatter. The more peaceful you are about others, the easier it is to be peaceful about yourself.

Journal Day 8:

Can you think of a time you heard a judgment made about someone else that ended up making you feel bad?

day 09

The blame game

I used to hold a lot of "truths" close to me that were not so true. I passed around a lot of blame for how I ended up in a state of self-hate. It was my genetics. It was "the world" and "society" and "magazines" and every other woman on the planet who were responsible for my hate. Family members, co-workers, bullies past and present, had said hurtful things. No question. There were a million places to point to "this is why I'm screwed up." Let me tell you, I was so talented at blaming others that the enemy had become pretty much everyone but me. Especially, other women. You know the ones. The ones who (I believed) had it all...the ones who didn't struggle, whose bodies were effortless, "I can eat anything I want and not gain weight" masterpieces? More specifically, the ones who my ex-boyfriends (who had, of course, dumped me) dated after me. Yes, I hated them. That is, I hated them with what little energy I had left after hating myself. When I turned the corner to self-love, I actually sent letters of apology to a few girls from college who I was less than friendly to because they were women I hated and blamed at the time.

Still, it all felt unfair. So unfair. What's worse, none of it felt within my control, so I decided I would just have to go on hating myself.

I'm sure I've received an incredible amount of compliments in my lifetime. But I internalized every criticism, adding it to the pile of people to blame for my self-worth.

The list of examples I could include here is exhaustingly long. But what I don't want to do is give you a list of clichés to consider, so here are a few of my personal examples.

It's amazing how easy it is to conger up these memories. I'm sure I've received an incredible amount of compliments in my lifetime. But I internalized every criticism, adding it to the pile of people to blame for my self-worth.

In college there were only a few nightlife options for the under 21 crowd. So my friends and I ended up at the same dance club on the same night and came to know all the other regulars. This particular club had an "amateur strip night" event (the only under 21 night, and the only viable under 21 dance night anywhere) followed by a regular dj and dancing. There was a group of older guys we ran into weekly who were very attractive. They were professional dancers who cleaned up the winnings each week at this event. They came off as a little sleazy (in hindsight their constant attention on the 18 year old club goers was perhaps unsavory in itself). But nonetheless they were all abs and gorgeous faces. While none of us were seriously interested in pursuing them, I think my friends understandably enjoyed their attention. Being as self-conscious as I was, I never talked to them. They regularly expressed interest in my friends, and

I would awkwardly hang to the side. I've always loved to dance, so I'd focus my attention there and avoid any interaction with the professional dancers. One night, the group had walked us to our car and were still attempting to convince my friends to hang out after hours. I was sitting in the back of the car, half paying attention as this song and dance always ended the same way and I was just ready to go home. I don't know what happened next, or how I became the topic of conversation, but I suddenly became aware that they were talking about me. It was like something out of an after-school special on self-esteem. They were laughing, pointing at me in the back and oinking like pigs.

I wanted to get out the car and run away crying. I was shocked at their behavior, but almost just as shocked they even knew I was alive. I was so convinced of my invisibility that this felt like an affront on multiple levels. Were these people I cared about? Not really. We don't exchange Christmas cards. I don't know their middle names or have relationships with their mothers. These guys remain insignificant in the grand scheme of my life. However the awful feeling that set in my stomach while they were laughing and oinking at me is one I will never forget. It's amazing how such a thoughtless action can remain with you for a lifetime.

That same year my grandmother came to visit me on my birthday. I know she loves me very much, but growing up she was always very critical of my body. I understand now that is a result of her lifelong criticism of herself. She grew up in an era of even more narrow confines of who and what women were allowed to be. Her judgment of me was meant to be loving, to help me become a good woman. But that realization didn't come until later adulthood. In the interim I would internalize every word.

I was very excited to show my grandma my new school. It was exciting to have a visitor, and it felt special that she would drive four hours just to take me to dinner for my birthday. She had some trouble finding my dorm so I was sitting outside waiting for her for a while. When she finally pulled up and got out of the car, I went running to greet her. We embraced and then she took a step back to look at me. I was expecting, "Happy birthday" or "It's so good to see you!" or even, "This place is a little confusing to navigate." But the first words out of her mouth were, "Oh honey! You've gained weight and your acne is flaring up!" Her tone drenched in concern, as I know for her the rest of that thought was, "How will she ever get a husband?"

I could keep going. There was the "boom-bada, boom-badas" as I walked across the classroom in 2nd grade. The boy who told me during my brief stint with thinness in jr. high (by way of starving myself) that he and the other boys "would totally like me if it weren't for my face," (presumably referring to the severe acne I had at the time)." The moniker "buffalo butt" I couldn't shake for the entirety of elementary school, which only lost momentum when Sir Mix-A-Lot's "Baby Got Back" suddenly popularized a larger derriere. And in more recent years, the female gym owner/trainer who spoke with me in my interview about the importance, specifically for female personal trainers of "looking the part."

This is not a pity party. But rather a means to illustrate that if you are angry at how others have treated you or been judgmental and rude with regards to your appearance, I certainly understand. I have an over-flowing filing cabinet in my mental rolodex marked "terrible things people have said to me." The misstep, however, was in placing my self-respect in others hands. As long as I held on to other's judgments, blaming them for how I felt about myself, I was unable to deal with my own feelings. If I waited for "everyone" to agree that I was wonderful and reflect that back at me in order to see myself clearly, I would be waiting forever.

While I in no way want to minimize any of your feelings of self-loathing, your self-perception is *not* outside of your control. I could write book after book after book about the beauty myth, the ever-changing standards of beauty, Photoshop, and the long-term psychological effects of bullying... but none of that would change the reality that the most important "voice in your head" is your own. So while being accountable for the voice in your head may feel like a burden to bear, your self-worth is wholly dependent on your own voice. This can be empowering! It means you are in the driver's seat and that while some of that burden may have been impacted by outside influences, your influence is greater. It is not "those voices" that weight you down, but rather "those voices" that become your own. And that, my friend, you can change. *Nothing and no one else has to change for you to change.* It takes work, but it is completely up to you.

Consider this: if I could wave a magic wand and completely remove every outside influence you could blame for your issues with your body and make them change in the exact way that you wanted or needed, it is highly likely you would still be left with a pile of your own baggage to sort through. Everything else could disappear, and you'd still be left with the way you bully yourself as the primary factor in your unhappiness. To my mind, it stands to reason that the way you bully yourself is not only the primary thing you have to change, it is also the most important.

I could write book after book after book about the beauty myth, the ever-changing standards of beauty, Photoshop, and the long-term psychological effects of bullying ... but none of that would change the reality that the most important "voice in your head" is your own.

Again, feeling guilty about this stuff is just another way to bully yourself. There is no room for guilt in making your move toward peace and acceptance. This is not about finding fault; it's about moving on.

Mindfulness Practice Day 9:

Who are you blaming for your current emotional and physical state? Spend at least 5 minutes journaling or thinking about it. Is it social media? Is it your mother? Your partner? Your kids? Ask yourself who or what you've been blaming. If you need to be mad today, fine. Be mad. Just begin unraveling the stories you've been telling yourself by figuring out what the story is and who you've been blaming.

Journal Day 9:

Let it fly. Make the list of everyone and everything to blame for how you feel about yourself. There's no right or wrong here. You cannot begin to let go of what you cannot acknowledge.

day *10*

Forgiveness

It's hard to talk about forgiveness without delving into religious ideologies. I don't want to do that. I do want to talk about forgiveness. I believe that forgiveness is in the interest of the forgiver (you) and less so the recipient. Forgiving those who you may feel keep you from believing in your own worth, is really a step in the direction of your self-acceptance. Holding onto blame, even when others' actions have been genuinely deplorable, doesn't leave you the space to heal and grow.

By now, I have revealed a few times that I have an ex-boyfriend who was critical of my weight. Whenever I have repeated his words that my weight was "bad for his reputation," people audibly gasp. The truth is, he is an old flame with whom it now makes complete sense that I am not long-term compatible. We shared a lot of life experiences together in our twenties. We share a lot of good memories. He is someone with whom I do not currently have a relationship, but for whom I hold a special place in my memories.

Forgiving those who you may feel keep you from believing in your own worth, is really a step in the direction of your self-acceptance. Holding onto blame, even when others' actions have been genuinely deplorable, doesn't leave you the space to heal and grow.

What he represents for me is paramount to my development. When he made that statement (which may never leave my mind), it was my kryptonite. I can quickly forget a billion positive compliments but somehow hold the criticism forever. In my case, I had long believed that something was seriously wrong with my body and I believed my "wrongness" was directly proportional to my worthiness of love.

We seek proof of our own perceptions. I found my greatest insecurity's perfect match in his overheard statement that I was bad for his reputation and therefore not worthy of love and commitment. Unless I changed my body. For this reason, I didn't question the relationship. I didn't ask myself if this was the person for me. I didn't wonder if his remark was kind or well intentioned. I didn't stand tall and state that I clearly would not be in any kind of relationship with someone who was afraid to acknowledge me in public. Instead I clung to him because I believed if I could somehow prove to him I was good enough then perhaps I would be. It is fair to say I was obsessed with the task of proving myself to him, as I failed to see my own inherent value.

In the end, I'm not sure what caused him to make that statement. I'm sure it's one he never meant for me to hear. Even if he had said it to my face, I'm certain he couldn't have explained why in a way that made sense. I could continue to be angry with him, to pick his statement apart, to deliberate on his character, to be pissed at him for my subsequent action of clinging to him like he held the key to my worth. Of course, none of that would serve me. I had to let go.

We don't always get to understand other people's actions. Sometimes in what seems a divine act of grace, we get clues or even apologies. Those stories of closure are rare. In truth, closure is something you can offer yourself when you choose to forgive. In my story, we've never spoken of these hurtful words. Perhaps in some odd twist of fate we'll talk about it someday and I'll get some closure. More important than closure, was forgiveness. What I needed to do to march closer to accepting myself in spite of his and anyone else's criticism was to forgive. I needed to reach deep down into the depths of my being and grant the kind of forgiveness that felt like unloading heavy bags from my shoulders.

I had to forgive him, as his words only hurt me because I agreed with them. I had to forgive him because holding on to that hurt did not allow me space to grow and move on. I needed to forgive *myself* for my reaction to his words and actions. I attached myself to someone else's words as though they were the complete truth of who I was. It was me who clung to those words, and as long as I maintained that he was the problem I would never hold myself accountable for my own voice.

My husband has never once been critical *or* complimentary of my weight. He loves me, he is proud of me, and he is clearly attracted to me. He loved me at my largest and at my smallest. Even though he was very proud for me when I met physical goals, like running my first half marathon, he never once praised my weight loss alone. It is abundantly clear to me that our relationship is in no way contingent on my appearance. Yet at the beginning of our relationship I was terrified he might leave me if I gained weight. It is perhaps arguable that this fear is the reason I did. I gained over 60 pounds in the first year of our relationship. As I've mentioned, I felt *awful* for him. I believed I couldn't possibly be attractive, let alone worthy of his attention if I wasn't thin. Even though these two relationships were completely different, I carried my values into each of them. While one reflected my insecurities back at me, the other supported me completely. In both cases, I was still left with an incredibly low sense of self-worth because in both cases, *I was still left to deal with me.* Just as my ex's unkind words couldn't "make me" feel bad about myself, my husband's support couldn't "make me" feel good. It was never up to anyone but me.

You deserve forgiveness. For all the ways you have hurt yourself. For all the truths you have accepted that were untrue. You deserve to forgive those who have hurt you so that you can dismiss the belief that it is they who need to change. Forgiveness is not excusing. It is not forgetting. It is letting go so that you may take one step closer to yourself. You will see; forgiveness buys you freedom from the opinions of others. You deserve that.

Mindfulness Practice Day 10:

Get out your list from yesterday. Spend some time in your head with all the people and things you've listed to blame for your harshly critical inner voice. Now, simply forgive them. Say a prayer if you are into that. Ask for the strength to let go of your anger and hurt. When or if you feel angry or sad, take a deep breath and consciously forgive. Take another breath and forgive yourself. Breathe in and out and forgive. Remember, forgiveness isn't about whether or not the person you've forgiven is deserving; it's about you being deserving of not carrying around that baggage anymore. Again, breathe in and out. Today is the day that you forgive so you can move on. You are on the path to taking responsibility for your own voice.

Journal Day 10:

Who do you need to forgive? How does it feel to think about doing so? This topic can bring up all kinds of stuff. Write it out of your system.

day *11*

Editing your experience

But Erin, I'm doing this work! I'm forgiving others. I'm beginning to forgive myself. I'm working on my old stories. But everywhere I look are messages to the contrary! How can I change my mind when the culture around me is bombarding me with how I need to change my body and my appearance?

Boy, do I get it. What I'm offering you is a new lens. Self-acceptance won't come without resistance, both from within yourself and from your outside influences. Many of your closest friends and family members will resist your change. As I came to reject the notion that my body was the property of others to be inspected or displayed for constant criticism, the people in my inner circle, even the people I love the most, offered resistance as I made these inner changes.

First I'll tell you that everyone in your life is comfortable with you the way you are today. The way you are right now. Everyone in your life is balanced around your current state, and if you change, there is a "rebalancing" of sorts that happens around you. Even if you change for the better. For example, a friend of mine recently called to tell me she was finally throwing in the towel on a relationship that was years old and years dead. She had been seeing this guy on and off forever. I offered her congratulations on her bravery in walking into the unknown, on her conviction to let go of what wasn't serving her and the tidbit of advice that she might find others in her life would initially resist her choice. She was surprised. She told me that everyone wanted her to move on. They would support her decision. I repeated that it would take time for them to adjust to the changes she was making. That while it was a positive change, her people were all comfortable with her as she was (with an ill-advised boyfriend) and would need time to rebalance.

She called me the next day and said my prediction had come true. Her (very supportive) mother had suggested that she call the dude and invite him along somewhere they were going as a family…right after she had told her mother about her break-up. Her mother wasn't being a jerk; she was unconsciously operating within her "old story" of her daughter. She didn't mean to be discouraging of her daughter's choice to move on. She surely hadn't meant to encourage the relationship she didn't believe was best for her. She simply had not changed to reflect her daughter's change. It takes time to do so.

When I made changes, both emotionally and with my physical body, I experienced wide backlash. From people I love dearly. In retrospect, they were just readjusting to who I was becoming. You might experience some strange behavior or resistance to your newly blossoming attitude toward yourself and others; know that your inner circle may change. Some of them will adjust and simply need time to do so. Some may leave you for a time and come back healthier (many of mine have). Just acknowledge that any change in YOU requires new behavior from others and lovingly allow them the space to adjust. They will. And if they don't, then that relationship was contingent upon you being miserable (too). In which case you may mourn, but to your betterment. Time will tell.

When I made changes, both emotionally and with my physical body, I experienced wide backlash. From people I love dearly. In retrospect, they were just readjusting to who I was becoming.

In terms of other influences, it may be time to turn the television off. I recently took three giant leaps away from mine. The longer I live this work and the more I affirm my own right to be me, the louder those "sweat is fat crying," or "you are only allowed to be a *work in progress*" messages feel. I do love (perhaps embarrassingly) some good television programs. I tend to like shows where women get to talk and do more than be pretty. Ironically, these shows are marketed to women and they are flooded with weight loss commercials, beauty commercials and constant messages about what I "should" do to be more attractive. They tell me "he" will notice me! That I will be beautiful! That my life will be better! And all I have to do is buy some product or consume some potion. Anymore, I don't even want to muster up the energy to refute it. I have turned my television off. I've found that the things I love most in my life are better served without it.

Social media is rampant with these messages. Mostly, again, they want to sell you magic things that make you different and amazing and happy. On social media these messages can be easier to limit. For example, if you have an annoying Facebook friend, simply click Hide. They will never know. It doesn't disavow your friendship, it just means they won't be in your newsfeed. If the messages that offend you are what I call "fitspiration" in the form of headless women with "motivational" bodies, click on Unlike. Social media, for me is not such a negative thing because you can edit your experience so easily. You can remove friends and messages that no longer serve you. It's liberating. It's freeing. It's freaking easy.

If a social media page is upsetting to your self-esteem, let it go. There are so many to choose from. If you want positive fitness messages, you can find those that don't post "ideal bodies" with suggestions to puke until you are beautiful. Let them go! You are likely finding them more irritating these days; it's okay to edit, unfriend, unlike and hide.

Mindfulness Practice Day 11:

Edit your experience. A lot of negative outside influences can be surgically removed from your life. That doesn't change your responsibility for yourself, but magazines, social websites, and media outlets are all things we consume purposefully. Don't buy the People magazine that rips apart women's "bathing suit bodies." Don't follow Facebook pages that only post headless women with quotes about killing yourself to be hot. There are lots of ways we have control over our experience. Take some time today to edit yours. Cancel subscriptions. Send emails to the Spam folder. Take control of your online and print experience.

Journal Day 11:

Who or what did you need to edit from your experience?

How does it feel to let them go? Are you anxious? Free?

day 12

Curating your life

Anytime is a good time to pay attention to where your energy is going. However, when you are in the midst of working on your mindset (which you are), this is a very important practice.

Where we put our energy is where we put our power.

We have a finite amount of energy and hours in every day. Where we put our energy is where we put our power. Where we put our energy is what grows. When I chose to spend so much of my energy picking myself apart, my disgust with myself grew. When I spend time with people who are negative all the time, I leave feeling negative. When I watch television or scroll through social media and see tons of feedback about how I should change, it takes energy away from me to engage. Energy that I cannot use for something else.

If you are thinking about how much you don't like something, you cannot also be thinking about what you love. If you are complaining about all the negative parts of your day, you cannot also be celebrating the moment you are in now. Energy is power. Energy is finite. Where yours goes reflects your character, your mood, and your happiness.

Energy is power. Energy is finite. Where yours goes reflects your character, your mood, and your happiness.

As we discussed in Chapter 11, editing your experience is important ... but curating is the fun part! What is curating? It's the sifting through, selecting, and organizing of the elements of your life and thoughts that you'd like to experience on a daily basis.

Now that you are lightening up the load a bit, quieting the voice of constant disapproval and letting go of messages that don't serve you, what influences do you *want* in your life?

Where would the right outside influences be the most helpful? It's time to decorate your life with what makes you happy, allow your energy to go there, and watch what grows!

This will look different for everyone. For me, it looks like little reminders around my house that I'm a bad-ass. I have Wonder Woman paraphernalia, a painting I created that says "I am deliberate and afraid of nothing" (an Audre Lorde quote), race medals I earned and "I love you" notes from my kiddo. I curate musical playlists for my different moods and use them during every workout and during every drive. I deliberately schedule times I can socialize with friends who I can rely on to be a loving influence. I go out dancing. I replace negative thoughts with positive ones. I follow social media pages about meditation, shame-free strength training advice, powerful women, parenting empowered girls, cute baby animals (who can be mad at cute baby animals?) and things that make me happy.

Nothing and no one can truly "make you happy." Happiness is a choice. In trying circumstances, sometimes peace is the next best thing. That said, filling my life and my experience with peaceful, uplifting, happy messages and objects is worthwhile and an uplifting gift to myself. It's one I feel grateful to myself for every day. It reminds me I'm worthy of great care. It's another way I take care of me.

Mindfulness Practice Day 12:

Beyond just editing, what would you add to your life/experience? What positive influences can you seek out as you work on changing your inner voice? Something as small as Post-it notes with meaningful messages left around the house can do a number on your mood. Find some social media sites (or images or quotes or music) that promote something you love or are passionate about: music, art, science, comedy, animals, sewing, Yorkies, books, your children. Seek out the doers, the folks who are living life and not just complaining about it. Influences are mostly chosen. Curate your experience.

Journal Day 12:

What did you add today? Is there anything you are just dying to add to your life online or otherwise that you cannot muster the courage to? What's keeping you from following your joy?

day *13*

Mirror, mirror on the wall

Believe me when I say that I realize nothing I'm asking you to do is easy. In more cases than not, we are talking about undoing decades of hurt and habit. A twenty-one day practice won't perform magic, but it could be a beginning should you choose it.

For me, experiencing love for my body was a non-negotiable goal. I didn't want to raise a little girl who hated her body and so I had to become a woman who was comfortable with and loving toward her own. I worked the concepts in this book. I quit saying aloud and wallowing in thought patterns that were detrimental. I spent time in my mirror actually looking at myself. I replaced thoughts about how gross I looked with thoughts that I was beautiful. *Even when I didn't quite feel it.* There is no wrong way to begin a more loving relationship with yourself. Where I'd like you to start today is in your mirror. Even, if not especially, if this has been a place you have gone to grieve.

I didn't want to raise a little girl who hated her body and so I had to become a woman who was comfortable with and loving toward her own.

To me, there is no rational argument that a human body would be worthy of disgust. If you believe in a creator, then that creator likely doesn't make mistakes. If you believe you simply came from your parents, what a beautiful place from which to emerge. You look like the two individuals who loved you into being. And if you don't have a relationship with your parents that would allow you to see them in the mirror looking back at you with love? Then your resilience alone makes you a knock-out. If one of us is beautiful then we're all beautiful.

I talk about beauty a lot. I don't believe it's "only on the inside" but that beauty is everywhere. We collect beautiful things to decorate our houses, our work environments, and even beautiful things in which to wrap our bodies. We seek out art and nature in an effort to experience beauty. To extend that lens to our physical bodies is a great gift – and it is doable.

I used to go to my mirror to mourn. I spent time there getting ready for the day. I would put on my make-up during my morning ritual but somehow did not "see" myself. I reserved looking at my body for horrifying moments under department store fluorescent lighting and there I would often cry. There I would suddenly look at myself as if for the first time and pick apart every detail. As much as I tried to tell myself that other parts of me (on the inside) were all that mattered, I couldn't really honor and respect all of me until I also accepted my body as my home. This never really dawned on me until I began taking a serious look at my behaviors and what I wanted for my daughter. I didn't want her to be a dissector of herself. I didn't want to teach her to be kind and loving yet abhor or disavow her physical self. I wanted her to see herself as I saw her…as a beautiful and complete being.

I often look to my daughter as my inspiration. I know that what I want for her is a reflection of the highest and purest part of me because I love her beyond any love I've ever known. What I want for her is pure, and I've come to understand that what I want for her is what I deserve for myself. I also know that I can only teach her what I embody and model. So I had to change my relationship with my mirror.

Sometimes I dance. Or I sit and puff my belly out and in. I grab at places I would have tried to hide in the past. I notice my skin. I notice how I'm built. I admire the curves of my shoulders and biceps. I keep looking until things seem less scary and more like home. I make myself laugh. I put on my best outfit. I make faces at myself. I allow negative thoughts to surface, notice them, and then replace them with something more loving. Even if I'm only going back to the Day 1 mantra: peace instead.

But why hang out in front of the mirror? Because everything looking back at you is your home. It's hard to work with it, be in it, or live in it, when you can't even look at it. It may feel weird or uncomfortable, but you deserve to feel at home in your body. Being able to look at it is a damn good place to begin.

Mindfulness Practice Day 13:

Spend at least five minutes at the beginning and end of your day in front of your mirror. Let old messages pop up and replace them with loving ones. Try, dear friend, to remember this body is your home. Begin to respect it. It has carried you a long way.

The only place to begin any journey is right where you are. So if this serves as a starting point for a journey toward better health and with it a changed body, then accept your starting point. There is only right now. This is the only body you have to live in today. It comes with its own beauty. There is always the possibility of peace. Begin to seek it.

Journal Day 13:

How do you feel in your mirror? How do you want to feel in your mirror? If you have a child, how do you want them to feel about their reflection?

day 14

Mantras

Mantras may seem a little new-agey or strange, but what you might not realize is that you already use them. Whatever you say to yourself every time something bad happens is a mantra. Whatever you automatically say to yourself when you look in the mirror is a mantra. The scripts we repeat about ourselves or the stories we believe to be truths about our lives are mantras. The trouble is, we believe our mantras are facts instead of realizing we created them.

Mantras I used to recite include, but aren't limited to:

- *If I wasn't fat this (insert awful thing) wouldn't happen to me.*
- *Other people have it so much easier.*
- *I can never be successful looking like this.*
- *If it's bad and can happen to me, it will.*
- *He will love me if I shrink.*

Or, probably the worst ones:

- *Everyone would be better off without me.*
- *I'm invisible and don't matter.*

Whew. Those last ones took a deep heavy breath to write. I now realize that those thoughts that infected my head when I experienced defeat, looked in the mirror or laid in bed at night were not real. They were thoughts I was *choosing.* Thoughts I had chosen so much they had become mantras. Mantras I'd repeated so often I was convinced they were facts.

So I made new mantras. In my case, I created mantras I hoped my daughter would come to own. I created mantras that were worthy of the life I wanted for myself instead of the life I'd convinced myself I was somehow doomed to live. What do you do with a mantra? Say it. Often. Remind yourself of it. Repeat it again. You can set an alarm on your phone and remind yourself of your mantra for the day. I think about my mantra before I work-out, when I'm brushing my teeth, when difficulties arrive and when I'm happy. Once you have a good one on "repeat" you'll think of it without meaning to. And just as crappy as thinking the same terrible things can make you feel, choosing something positive that resonates with you has equal and opposite effects.

It can be a quote that resonates. It can be something beautiful you were reminded of that inspired you. Again, this is your practice. It's about being loving. There is no wrong way to cultivate a loving practice toward yourself.

Some of mine you are welcome to borrow for inspiration:

- *All there is, is love. Where there isn't love, there is desperately seeking it. All there is, is love.*
- *I am worthy, I am strong, my voice matters.*
- *I can choose peace. There is always peace.*
- *There is beauty everywhere if I choose to see it.*

And sometimes it's:

- *I am powerful.*
- *I am love.*
- *I am light, or, simply,*
- *I am.*

As time goes on these continue to evolve for me. My personal theory is that self-actualization comes in three phases. Acceptance, peace and love. At any point you can be moving through these. You will unlikely simply "attain" love and then just remain there. But love cannot come without peace, and peace cannot come without acceptance. As I find myself spending less time working to accept myself, and more time choosing peace and love (even when making changes for my growth, it is possible to understand your weaknesses and work on yourself without doing so from a disparaging place), my mantras become even more empowering. "I can choose peace" doesn't come up as often as "I believe in miracles" these days. In fact, 6 years into living these practices, I very rarely give myself a "body love" pep talk. Because (a stark difference from who I once was) I have changed my values and accept myself as I am. Weight gain no longer feels like an assault on my worth or an epic failure. But these changes took time. Start where you are at. Allow yourself to evolve.

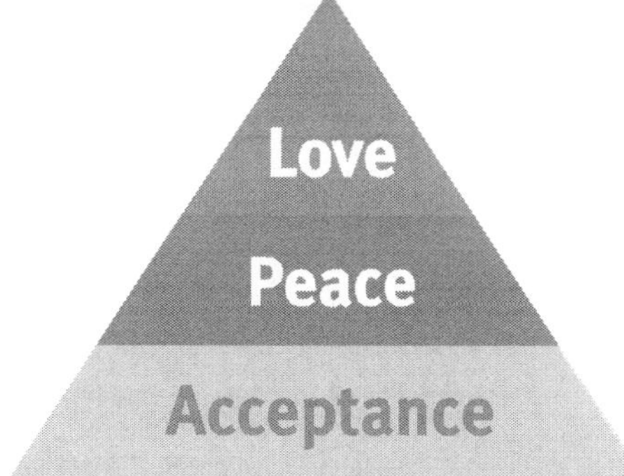

Mindfulness Practice Day 14:

Choose a mantra for the day. Repeat it to yourself as you brush your teeth, as you arrive at work, at meal times, before bed and any time your thoughts move away from love. It will likely feel forced at first. But your mantras become your inner voice. What feels awkward now will become the voice that guides you to a more loving place. If you are open to it, this can be a beautiful daily practice.

Journal Day 14:

Make a list of possible mantras. Feel free to steal from me or google. Just write what feels good.

day *15*

Moving

It may seem counter-intuitive to prescribe exercise to a person who is learning to love her (or his) body "as is," but there are few practices as useful for loving your body "as is" than exercise.

In the past, when I thought about working-out, I envisioned headless, dehydrated models emblazoned with quotes about never giving up. I pictured sweat and torture and getting *RESULTS*! I thought about protein powder and vanity and spandex. In short, I thought about a whole world that I didn't feel I belonged in, and it sounded like "body-fixing" torture. The precise torture I *should* be signing up for because then everything wouldn't be wrong with me. Cue guilt.

I'm not alone. Lots of people associate body "fixing" with torture and exercise. I believe that's the reason it is so "hard" to make a commitment to exercise and keep it. All these stories we tell ourselves about movement make it hard to stick with it. It makes me so sad.

This is what you need to know about movement and exercise:

Movement is empowering. Movement is exhilarating. Movement reduces stress. Movement is head-clearing. Movement releases happy hormones. Movement boosts self-esteem. Movement brings you to the present moment. Movement is an important part of respecting and caring for yourself. Human bodies and minds thrive on it and evolved to do it daily.

If all of that is hard to believe, *read it again.* I don't know you and I've no interest in lying to you. You might have to trust me on this one. At one point in time, I wouldn't have believed me either. But I would be remiss if I didn't let you in on this secret. I was so angry when I discovered that my issues with mood, depression, over-thinking and stress could all be successfully managed by *moving* daily. Why hadn't anyone told me? It clears my head. It allows me to let go of yesterday so today can be better. It gives me time and space alone. It's literally what keeps me afloat. Here I had spent years avoiding it. Go figure.

Movement is empowering. Movement is exhilarating. Movement reduces stress. Movement is head-clearing. Movement releases happy hormones. Movement boosts self-esteem. Movement brings you to the present moment. Movement is an important part of respecting and caring for yourself. Human bodies and minds thrive on it and evolved to do it daily.

I had tried working out. I remember a summer in college where I lost something like thirty pounds. I devised all of these "rules" for my dieting behavior, the most painful of which was that I had to work-out before eating each day. I viewed exercise as a punishment. I would go for a run while ruminating on how disgusting I found myself. If I had to walk a while, I would belittle myself for failing to run the whole way. I found none of my progress positive. I used the entire time to ridicule myself for the shape I was in. Nothing was ever good enough. I not only hated *what* I was doing but *how* I did it. Of course it was really just bullying on my part. It's no wonder these habits didn't "stick." I hated myself. I hated myself while exercising (and on a boat, and on a train). I hated the activities I chose and I hated how slow the visible physical results were. My attitude announced that movement was punishment.

As I began to move lovingly toward taking care of myself, I started to explore activities I might enjoy. I looked for opportunities to celebrate and take pride in the smallest victories, like getting out the door. For me, it started with walks around the block and soon expanded into an array of activities I now love. I literally evolved from believing I hated exercise and it just wasn't meant for me, to relishing my daily exercise as a nourishing and essential time to connect with myself.

In terms of my body image, there is nothing better for me than a great work-out. That has nothing at all to do with anticipated results and everything to do with the immediate great feeling I get from moving my body. I can walk into the gym feeling like a blob of body and leave feeling like a superstar athlete. Now that's an immediate transformation!

Also, being active forces you to connect with your body as your home. You have to be present in it, pay attention to its signals, and listen. Coming back home to your body and learning to listen to it will benefit you in so many ways, and it's the only safe way to exercise. If it *hurts* (hurting is different than the feeling of challenging yourself with exertion), stop. If it feels good, keep going.

Mindfulness Practice Day 15:

Plan to move for at least 10 to 20 minutes today. Don't get too caught up in what that movement is. I started with walks around the block and those turned into training for long races. It doesn't matter where the starting point is or what movement you choose, just move. The only rule is to find something you might enjoy, and focus on how it feels to enjoy movement. If you've no idea what you might enjoy you'll need to experiment. Let go of whatever old stories you have about what it means to move, what you can and can't do, or what the "results" are supposed to be. You deserve to treat your human body with respect. You deserve to clear your head and do something for yourself. You deserve your own time. You deserve movement. Let it be about that.

Journal Day 15:

How did you move today? How did it feel? If it didn't feel good, what might you try in an effort to find movement you enjoy? If it did, what is keeping you from that feeling? How did you feel before and after? Write it out.

day 16

Getting loud

One of my favorite ways to use movement constructively is to do what I call "getting loud." I get loud when I feel small, when I need to find my voice, and sometimes just because it's Tuesday.

Getting loud is a way I think about movement that makes me feel powerful, resilient and like I could conquer anything. I'm talking about exercise, but you might notice that I don't sound like a gym commercial. For me, exercise has nothing to do with fixing my body and everything to do with my mental and physical health. What keeps me doing it daily is how it makes me feel, not the promise of more attractive thighs. I'm not inherently opposed to such goals, but perhaps due to the magnitude of my former self-loathing for me they aren't enough of a motivator to continue my habits. But whatever your goals are, it's worth considering the other benefits of exercise so as not to miss them. These ideas can only add to your practice.

Getting loud is a way I think about movement that makes me feel powerful, resilient and like I could conquer anything.

The obvious way I get loud is to crank up some hip-hop in my ear-buds and do some strength training in the gym. I almost always walk into the gym feeling like a sad sack of morning, just because it's *way* early and I've usually not even spoken to anyone yet. I put on a powerful playlist, work myself at a challenging, boob-sweat inducing pace, and soon I begin to feel like a beast. (A good beast). I've often said, everything seems easier when you've chosen to do burpees before most of the world rises.

A less obvious way I use movement to feel powerful is walking. Years ago, walking would not have made my list of "go-to" activities. Walking conjures up an image of senior citizens power-walking around the mall in orthopedic shoes. While I fully intend to be one of those people one day, the idea of going for a walk to feel "powerful' didn't really fit with this picture.

Studies show that just a ten minute walk can do wonders for lifting your mood. It's hard to argue with ten minutes. I think I could probably come up with as many names for walking as Eskimos have for snow. A powerful walk for me is one where I do the following pose and meditation:

First, I walk with the sort of pace and "don't mess with me" attitude I adopt when I find myself walking to my car alone at night. My "keys prepared to attack" walk. Shoulders back, chest up, strong. Then I focus on softening my gaze and opening my heart. Thus keeping the strength but dropping the defensiveness. I notice the shifts in my energy as I work through this routine. Few things feel "louder" to me than my personal power walking meditation. This is usually coupled with a particularly powerful song (often the poet/rapper Dessa for me). Starting my day this way impacts every subsequent part of my day positively.

You don't have to become a boxer or do plyometrics at dawn to feel powerful. There are more ways than I can count. (If you don't know what a burpee is, now would be a good time to look it up!) Having my personal arsenal of powerful movements is a tool that keeps me sane. In those days and moments when I feel small or invisible, I pull out one of these techniques and take care of myself. I'm really not sure how I got by before I had these tools. I'm so happy to share them with you.

Mindfulness Practice Day 16:

Use movement today to get loud with yourself. Do something intentionally to feel powerful. Some suggestions; kick boxing (a DVD is fine), strength training, stair climbing, sprints, plyometrics, walking, or archery! Heck - just punch something or lift something heavy! Experiment today with how movement can make you feel powerful. Let it be about the feeling so you can call upon it when you need to. (Please don't hurt yourself). This is not about over-exerting yourself so much as standing your ground. It's the intention that makes all the difference.

Journal Day 16:

When do you lose your power or need it the most? When do you feel most powerful?

day 17

Getting quiet

The first year of my exploration of movement was mostly about getting loud. I had a baby at home, which offered lots of quiet time. Rocking, singing to and soothing a baby requires calm energy on a constant basis. Somehow changing poopy diapers did not make me feel strong and powerful. Back then, I needed to feel powerful in my time alone in a way that I need less often now. I still seek and find power in my regular movement routines, but as I've evolved I've found what I need more of now is quiet.

Currently, I have a lot going on in my life. I have a day job. I write. I have side job, a family, and a lot of balls in the air. Each of my responsibilities requires a different energy; chaos in any one of them can easily seep into the others. I'm not a "glorifier of busy," but chasing my passion involves supporting it. In order to face each day with the kind of peace and strength and clarity I desire to approach it with, I seek quiet in my exercise and alone time.

I stumbled upon this knowledge after I began taking my runs in the woods. I try to make my workouts about how I feel, so I pay attention to any urges or desires I have when I'm moving about. I began to notice a desire to stop and walk for a bit. I found a clearing in the woods that spoke to me and I began stopping there during every run to check in with myself. I would do a brief meditation. I'd often end up crying there if I needed an emotional release, sometimes from stress, sometimes from joy and most recently from gratitude. Lately I've also been leaving my earbuds at home to tune into the world around me.

You've probably gathered by now that I'm an emotional woman. I've resisted this fact most of my life because I perceived it as a huge character flaw. Now I realize that noticing, experiencing, and articulating emotions is a great strength. When mismanaged, certainly, it can be a weakness. Your weaknesses are just that, strengths mismanaged. This quieting or grounding practice has been so beneficial to me in managing my emotions in a productive, beautiful and purposeful way.

I also have a history of depression. I once spent so long locked in my room (in a basement apartment with no natural light) that my roommate locked me out of the house in a beautiful act of love and friendship. In college, after failing out of my classes for not attending, I was briefly medicated for both depression and anxiety. It was brief because I quickly rejected the side effects and stopped taking the medication which, I realize now, resulted in another downward spiral. This was a bleak time in my life. It's one I'm committed to not revisiting, but it takes a lot of self-awareness and care to avoid. Winter months, with less light and outdoor activity, are harder on me.

I'm open about all of this because I now know these problems are much more common than I realized, and because there are times everyone feels that their lives are spiraling out of control. Life throws us curve balls. Unfortunately, most of us can be pretty darn good at creating challenges for ourselves. I have discovered that spending some time at the beginning of the day checking in with myself keeps all my depression issues at bay. Instead of burying my struggles, I address them head on. This leaves me free to be present in my day and not stuck in old stories or yesterday's problems. Getting "quiet" with my movement has been the most effective way for me to heal myself.

**Everyone is different. If you struggle with depression it's imperative that you find what works best for you.

Getting quiet doesn't always look or feel the same. Hikes and runs in the woods are always therapeutic. I use that time to clear my head and deal with what comes to the surface. Yoga and stretching are very calming to me. Any activity I can do on or near the water feels peaceful. With my intention focused properly, even the weight room can become a quiet place where I find solace to begin the day. Remember, setting a different intention for a particular activity can make any practice soothing.

We bring all our baggage with us everywhere. (Wherever you go, there you are.) Getting quiet in a purposeful way is a great technique to unpack some lost luggage and move forward. Both staying the same and dealing with yourself require work, but both don't result in growth. Getting quiet will keep you moving and growing.

I use that time to clear my head and deal with what comes to the surface.

Mindfulness Practice Day 17:

Use movement today to get "quiet" with yourself. Turn everything off. Go for a walk. Head outside if you have access to a trail or a river or even the neighborhood trees. Stretching or yoga are good, too. Use movement to quiet your mind and find calmness. Let it be about the feeling so you can call upon it when you need to.

Journal Day 17:

When do you need quiet the most? What helps you feel quiet? What mantras are helpful when quieting your mind? What music brings you quiet peace? How can this practice serve you in your life?

day *18*

Feeding yourself

Nutrition is a really lovely concept when it is considered apart from the world of dieting. Just like exercise has a branding problem, healthy food does too. So much so that I was actually irate when I figured out how good it felt to feed my body well. Again, why hadn't anyone ever told me? I felt vibrant! I felt energetic! I felt...healthy?! Why did eating healthy have such a bad reputation and involve words like rabbit food, unappealing sounding foods like wheat germ and eating clean (sounds so sterile)?

Even after my revelation about the joys of healthful eating, my habits didn't change overnight, and it took time to figure out what felt and tasted best to me.

So this is a strange analogy but I like to compare food experimentation to alcohol experimentation. Adults who choose drink alcohol and have a healthy relationship with alcohol usually have followed a type of experimentation process.

Often, people have a drink of choice – say tequila or vodka, wine or beer. Individuals know how different amounts of their favorite drink will affect them – and they stop at one or two or three. These folks have discovered through trial and error what drinks don't work for them at all. Some drinks leave them feeling sick regardless of the amount, and some have lesser effects the morning after. Maybe these folks avoid certain kinds of alcohol because they find they become angry or volatile when they consume.

When it comes to drinking we don't insist that everyone else embrace our favorite drink. A "beer person" is a "beer person" and a "wine person" is a "wine person" and we respect that each person has figured that out for themselves. Even the "after care" (for me an electrolyte drink takes care of any issues the day after a drink of choice, in my case usually whiskey) usually has a specific recipe. In the case of alcohol (and for the life of me I cannot seem to find any other example so clear as this) we have an understanding of how what we consume effects our bodies. Furthermore, that these effects are individual. I believe food ought to be dealt with the same way. Through trial and error, experimentation and observation. And no judgment! Vodka people don't judge scotch people! What we consume has immediate and long-term effects on our body. It is worthwhile to figure those out and do what is best for us without extending our conclusions to others without regard for how individual these outcomes are.

In the past I had so many stories in my head about food and none of them served me well. "I deserve this," I would think before eating something that made me feel physically terrible. I chose to eat cookies and pizza and things I knew weren't doing my body any favors and then not enjoy the experience because I felt so damn guilty about it. I overate to comfort myself. I then under-ate to assuage my guilt from eating too much. I wasn't really listening to my body. All of these things contributed to a horrible disconnect between my head and the needs of my body as well as a lack of positive health outcomes.

I wasn't really listening to my body. All of these things contributed to a horrible disconnect between my head and the needs of my body as well as a lack of positive health outcomes.

It might seem kind of infuriating that I'm not handing out a nutrition plan in this book. After all, that's what we have been conditioned to believe that we need. I won't do that because I believe that when we are truly connected with our bodies, we make food choices that serve us well. I believe we will know for ourselves what foods sit well and what foods don't, what foods provide great energy and what foods don't. While there is nothing wrong with guiding principles for nutrition, I believe that *feeling* good is the best (and most effective, long-term) reason to choose your foods.

As for guiding principles, some people feel dramatically dif-

Eating to feel good, rather than to fix myself, is what led to me losing all the weight.

ferent preparing and eating whole, unprocessed foods. Others feel really good eating portions that sustain their energy without overstuffing and feeling bloated. Once experimenting, many people find there are foods that they are sensitive to that they had no idea effected them negatively. Taking the time to figure out those variables for myself was a surprising, enlightening and worthwhile process. Eating to *feel* good, rather than to fix myself, is what led to me losing all the weight.

In the nutrition world, misinformation and judgments abound. It's unfortunate because good food is out there. There is good information available and ultimately your body will tell you what's right for you – if you listen. What we put in our bodies becomes part of us. It's worthwhile to figure out what works best for you.

Mindfulness Practice Day 18:

Be mindful of how you feel after eating today. Are you ready for a run or a nap? Do you feel sleepy? Before you chose your meal, did you think about how it would make you feel? What might you have chosen if you were thinking about feeling energized all day?

Allow yourself the benefit of your own wisdom about your body and, as you feel ready, experiment with different food choices. This one is certainly not a one-day practice. You can start it today, however. How does eating make you physically feel? How do different choices affect your feelings? The more you can be curious about your results and outcomes, the more likely you are to make clear and compassionate choices.

This practice shouldn't be about a diet or guilt, about *being* good or bad; it's about feeling good.

Journal Day 18:

How does it feel to think about food as something that can make you feel good? Does what you eat now lend to feeling good? What emotions come up when you are thinking about food? How do you want to feel about food?

day 19

Food and feelings

I had heard the term "emotional eater" for years before I realized I might be one. Sure, I'd eaten ice cream when I was sad before, but that seemed normal. It wasn't until I started eating healthfully that I noticed my own pattern.

First, understand that a regular day of eating for me includes a lot of produce. I plan all of my meals and snacks in advance (a process that I thought was time consuming but have since found saves tons of time since it keeps me from scrambling every time I'm hungry). I enjoy indulgences as I choose, but for the most part my eating habits are pretty routine. None of those routines are as unwavering and unchanging as my breakfast.

Every day for at least a year I've had sprouted grain bread with lemon juice and avocado for breakfast. I eat this every day unless (God forbid!) I run out of something. I've found through trial and error that this combination leaves me feeling full and nourished until lunch time, or longer if the day gets away from me. I never need more.

One day, *after eating my breakfast*, I encountered my husband in our bathroom. He was getting ready for work. I said "good morning" to him. He didn't respond. I repeated myself. Still no response. I said "busy day ahead?" Nothing.

Now, in my rational mind, I know my husband could not hear me. He's the kind of person that needs to ready himself and drink a cup of coffee before anyone or anything exists. It's not personal. But apparently I wasn't being rational in that moment. Because the next thing I did was walk into the kitchen and begin to pull open the cabinets, mindlessly looking for something to eat.

It was almost hilarious to me when I finally paused to actually notice what I was doing. Was I hungry? Er, no. I had just consumed the breakfast that sustains me *every single day*. It was then I realized, like a slap on the face, that I was feeling invisible and unimportant and had come to eat away those feelings. I *was* an emotional eater. Me.

I put down the box of snacks. I walked back into the bedroom. I told my husband (who evidently was able to hear me this time) that I had felt ignored and so I commenced to eat everything in the kitchen but managed to stop myself. As he stared sort of dumbfounded at me, having no idea what I was talking about, I proceeded to say, "I just needed to say that aloud to someone. I know you can't hear me before coffee."

This is a perfect example of a pattern I suddenly realized I always had. Whenever I felt insignificant, I overfed myself. I sort of knew that's what I was doing when I would buy Ben and Jerry's after a break-up, and in my new-found, body-conscious reality I was able to identify that this was a much more frequent pattern than even I had realized.

These days, I just ask myself if I am hungry before I eat.

It's a pretty simple task. Am I hungry? No? Is something wrong? It's pretty simple, but it makes a world of difference.

Mindfulness Practice Day 19:

Just for today, ask yourself if you are feeding your hunger or something else. Are you feeding your insecurity? Your perceived insignificance? Your worry? Your feelings of hopelessness? The simple act of asking yourself if you are hungry can go a long way in understanding your behavior. In the end, being curious and non-judgmental about your own behavior is the best way to change it. What are you feeding?

Journal Day 19:

Are you an emotional eater? How long have you had these behaviors? How does it feel thinking about them? What if eating was only a positive experience? What would that look like?

day 20

All there is, is love

It has been said that all emotions can be boiled down to either love or fear. Perhaps this is just my rose-colored glasses, but I think you can reduce fear and love down to just … love. I believe everything I encounter is either love itself or an act of desperately seeking it. From someone opening a door for me to someone flipping me off in the car, all I see is love or seeking it. This is the lens I use personally to comprehend others and, more importantly, myself.

I believe everything I encounter is either love itself or an act of desperately seeking it.

When I'm choosing something for myself, I try to always do so from a place of love. From relationships to food choices to my inner dialogue, I have the power every day to make choices from love or from a place of desperately seeking love.

It is always up to me.

"All there is, is love" is a mantra I have displayed everywhere. It's on my planner. (Yes, I still have a planner.) It's on my Post-its. It's what I remind myself of when someone is attacking me in person (verbally) or online and it's what I truly believe. It's where I turn when I find myself lapsing back into patterns of despair. It's more than knowing that I deserve love, it's a fundamental belief that anything other than love is an utter illusion. Usually one I've created.

It's more than knowing that I deserve love, it's a fundamental belief that anything other than love is an utter illusion. Usually one I've created.

But what about mean people, you ask? What about those jerks who ________ (fill in the blank)? I view these so-called jerks as folks desperately seeking love, sometimes they need validation and sometimes they need to drag others through the mud. It's all love-seeking. Some of it more dysfunctional than others. Just remember that we choose who we let take our energy and to what we give our attention. So I don't put my energy there. It doesn't really help me or the other person to dissect or over-analyze their perhaps careless behavior. To do so simply adds energy and momentum to the negativity. I focus all my energy on love.

I want to be able to say: "I was bold. I loved hard. I did what I believed in."

To that end, I just can't stand in my mirror being sad or upset anymore. I don't want to try on clothes for hours to find something in which I feel skinny enough. I don't want to hide my face or hide behind cloaks. I have a full, amazing life. I have exciting plans for my future. I want to make a mark on the world. I want to go out blazing, with my fist in the air. I want to be able to say: "I was *bold*. I loved hard. I did what I believed in."

I gotta say, there just isn't any room in that vision statement for me to worry about how my thighs look while I'm making history. Not only am I more valuable than that, it's actually boring. It serves no purpose, brings me no closer to perfection, and honestly doesn't align with my personal values.

I don't agree that I am here to be admired. I don't agree that my job is to "be healthy!" by doing everything in my power to look different than I do today. When I think about how I want to spend my time and energy, about what I truly value for my life, my weight simply does not make the cut. Not even close.

Nothing I have ever accomplished that really mattered had anything at all to do with my body, unless it was about something it had DONE. My body has given birth. It has crossed finish lines. It has climbed mountains. Those are the things that matter to me.

I don't agree that I am here to be admired. I don't agree that my job is to "be healthy!" by doing everything in my power to look different than I do today. When I think about how I want to spend my time and energy, about what I truly value for my life, my weight simply does not make the cut. Not even close.

My body is not perfect. Just yesterday, I was at my body-worker's office and became tearful about something that made me feel unworthy. For a whole day I felt like a mess, and fell right into my old "I'm invisible and unworthy of love" story. It's not like you can make all your junk magically go away overnight. But you can name it. You can notice it immediately when it arises, and you can address it. Your old stories don't have to be your forever story. It's up to you. I believe in love. I believe I deserve it. I believe you deserve it. And I believe it's all there really is. What would happen if you let love rule your life? What would change if you stopped asking, "Am I beautiful enough" and started asking, "Am I living a beautiful life?"

Mindfulness Practice Day 20:

Where are your thoughts? Are they loving or desperately seeking love? Today, consider today thinking about what you value for your life. Is it love? Success? Family? Does the way you choose to spend your energy and the subject matter of your thoughts reflect this? If not, it may be time to start living more congruently with your personal values. And that begins with how you choose to spend your energy, today.

Journal Day 20:

Do you find your thoughts are mostly negative or positive? How does your thought pattern serve you? Which of the practices you have tried have been most helpful in changing your thought patterns in a positive way? How can you further integrate those into your life?

day 21

Do your best

In short, I've asked you to make a total paradigm shift away from the cultural norm. I've asked you to completely change your inner voice and perceptions and to do so in 21 days. I know that's not really how this business works. I know that 21 days isn't a magical length of time. I know that for any of this to work, it is up to you to internalize, reflect, and consciously change. So perhaps you keep revisiting the days that give you the most challenge. Maybe you stretch these 21 days into a year or half a year. Your inner work is your own, so while I hope to offer some nuggets to help you along, this process will ultimately be completely unique to you.

I'd like to leave you with the charge to do your best. I know that my daily best is not always better than the day before. Significant change usually comes with resistance and even back-sliding. It doesn't happen perfectly (the way we want or expect) and it doesn't happen overnight. But what stands between us and a better relationship with our lives, is the relationship we have with ourselves. While it's hard to change, I promise it's much harder to stay the same.

I believe you deserve your own time, love and respect. I believe when you realize this too, your life will reveal itself to you in ways you couldn't have imagined before, because you hadn't believed yourself worthy. That's not the promise at the end of the weight loss rainbow, that's the promise at the end of the self-respect rainbow.

Mindfulness Practice for Every Day:

Do your best. Be compassionate with yourself. Each day's best may not be better than the last. Allow yourself to fall down; help yourself back up and keep moving forward. It is possible to strive to be better and not kick yourself every time you fall down. The trick is to be a compassionate friend to yourself. You deserve that.

I believe you deserve your own time, love and respect. I believe when you realize this too, your life will reveal itself to you in ways you couldn't have imagined before, because you hadn't believed yourself worthy. That's not the promise at the end of the weight loss rainbow, that's the promise at the end of the self-respect rainbow.

Made in the USA
Middletown, DE
08 February 2016